The world in which Jesus lived sometimes seems very remote from our modern age, but his family life was not really so different from that of a child of today. His father worked, and his mother looked after them both, worrying when things went wrong, and proud of her son, just as a modern mother would be. Here, told simply for everyone to understand, is the warmly human story of Jesus, the man who was the Son of God.

LADYBIRD BOOKS LTD
0 7214 7511 6

SCRIPTURE UNION
0 85421 886 6

THE LIFE OF JESUS

by JENNY ROBERTSON

illustrated by ALAN PARRY

Ladybird Books Loughborough

Scripture Union London

THE CHILDHOOD OF JESUS

In a little home in a quiet town called Nazareth, dinner was cooking. Beans and yellow peas bubbled in the pot. Mary was making barley bread. Suddenly a voice called her name. She looked up, amazed. . . A stranger stood beside her. Light shone from his face. 'The Lord is with you, Mary,' he said. 'God is pleased with you. He is giving you a baby boy whose name is to be Jesus. . . He is the promised king who saves his people, the Son of God.'

At first Mary was puzzled and afraid but then she said, 'I am the Lord's servant maid. I will do whatever he wants.'

Many people in Nazareth said unkind things when they knew Mary was going to have a baby before she was married. She was engaged to Joseph, the carpenter. At first Joseph thought he should not marry Mary after all, but God spoke to him in a dream telling him to marry Mary. Joseph did what God told him. He married Mary and they were very happy, while they waited for the baby to be born.

'The Romans who rule our country want everyone to travel back to the towns where their families first lived. They are trying to count everyone in our country so that they can tax them. Mary, my dear, this will mean a hard journey for you; Bethlehem, my family's town, is such a long way away,' said Joseph, anxiously.

'God will look after us,' Mary said.

It was a very long journey. The rocky road wound through the hilly countryside.

'There we are! Nearly there now!' Joseph pointed to the little walled town on the hill ahead.

'I am so glad,' Mary said. 'Won't it be nice to sleep inside tonight! We've slept out in the open so often, with only the little fire you light to keep the wild beasts away. It will be much safer to rest at an inn with other people. I shall be glad to lie down! My baby will be born very soon.'

'Then we must hurry on! Do you see how bare the hills are? King David looked after his father's sheep here long ago. Our teachers say that Bethlehem, David's town, is the place where the promised king will be born,' said Joseph. 'Hurry, little donkey! God is looking after us. The teachers have told the truth. Our baby king will be born tonight in royal Bethlehem!'

But Bethlehem was crowded. 'No room! No room!' the innkeeper cried.

'Please,' Mary begged, 'everywhere is full. Can't you help at all?'

'I wish I could, dear! Wait a minute, though. Look. . . this way! You can sleep in the stable. The straw's clean and the cows will keep you warm.' He turned to Joseph. 'Hurry, friend. . . the ground will be soft enough, heaped with hay.'

So Jesus was born that night in a stable, because there was no room anywhere else for him in royal Bethlehem.

No one in the crowded, busy town knew that God's promised Son lay in the inn stable, but an angel brought the news to some shepherds who were guarding their sheep in the hills outside Bethlehem. 'News, good news for everyone!'

The shepherds looked up, terrified. More and more shining messengers, brighter than the starlit sky, crowded round them.

'Don't be afraid,' said one. 'Your promised king, your Saviour, has been born close by in Bethlehem. You'll find him wrapped in linen cloth, lying in a manger. Go quickly and see!'

Then the shepherds heard the angels singing, 'Glory to the most high God, peace to his people on Earth.'

The startled shepherds left their sheep and hurried over the hillside to Bethlehem.

Trying to tiptoe, they crowded into the stable and peered into the manger where Jesus slept on the hay. They felt very happy as they told Mary and Joseph about the shining messengers, their songs and their good news.

When they saw the tiny baby they whispered joyfully, 'Oh, praise God! Thank God! He has sent this newborn baby to be the Saviour of our people. The promised king has come at last. He is not born in a

king's palace, but in a stable. God has come to us, his poor people!'

They hurried away to tell everyone the news, while Mary sat and watched her baby boy.

'It's dark in the stable. The cows moo and stamp. The donkey's breath warms you. Rats run about in the hay, but the music of highest heaven plays for you, dear Jesus. Sleep well, little one, sleep well,' Mary murmured.

Far away in the east a bright star blazed night after night, drawing wise men riding on their camels closer and closer to Bethlehem. Each dry, hot day they rested, shaded by their kneeling camels. At night they rode on, following the bright star. The cold wind stung their faces as they gazed at the sky.

'The star tells me a king is born. I am old, yet when I saw the star I left my home and my books to follow it,' said one.

'It must be guiding us to the royal palace. We will certainly find the baby there! The star tells me the newborn child is to be a king of wonder who will rule for ever.'

Cruel King Herod welcomed the wise men to the palace but their news alarmed him.

'A star tells these visitors that a wonderful king is born in *my* kingdom!' Herod thought. He turned to the priests who stood near him. 'Where is the promised king to be born?' he asked.

'In Bethlehem, O king!' the Jewish priests bowed, hating this foreign ruler of theirs who did not know that Bethlehem was the town where God had promised that his special king should be born.

'I must get rid of this baby!' thought Herod. '*I* am king in this land.' He told the wise men, 'Search for the child in Bethlehem. Tell me where to find him. I wish to bow before him also,' he lied.

The wise men found Mary and Jesus in a little house in Bethlehem.

'Here is gold for the King of kings,' said one.

'I have brought sweet-smelling frankincense. I worship God in this small child,' another bowed low.

'Little King, I give you myrrh, for you will heal many hurts, yet you too will suffer greatly,' said a third, gravely.

Mary wondered what they meant, but already danger threatened their baby. That night God warned Joseph of Herod's plans to kill the baby king. 'You must take Mary and the child to Egypt,' God told Joseph. 'You will be safe there.'

Mary and Joseph got ready at once. They tied their bundles onto the little donkey's back and, carrying their baby, escaped from King Herod's cruel soldiers. They did as God had told Joseph and went far away to Egypt. There they lived happily until wicked King Herod died and it was safe for them to go back home to Nazareth.

So Jesus grew up in Nazareth. He loved helping Joseph in the carpenter's shop.

'That's fine, Jesus! Hold that end steady now,' smiled Joseph.

'We're working hard!' Jesus called to Mary. She smiled at her son. He was growing up so sturdy and strong. No one here in little Nazareth knew anything about the star, or the wise men with their strange, costly gifts. That was their secret. She thought about it sometimes, especially when Jesus did or said things that surprised her, as happened when he was twelve years old. He and his parents, with other families from the village, had travelled all the way to Jerusalem for the Passover festival.

It was wonderful to climb the steep narrow streets to the golden Temple! Long after the other families from Nazareth had left, Jesus stayed on. He spoke to the wise teachers who studied the holy writings that taught about God.

'Who is this boy?' the learned men wondered. 'He knows the writings that tell of God's promises but, even more, he knows God himself in a special way. He is completely at home here in God's house.'

'Jesus!' Joseph tiptoed in. 'Your mother and I have searched for you for two days!'

'Why have you done this to us?' Mary asked. 'We've been so worried about you.'

'Didn't you know I must learn my Father's ways?' Jesus answered, but he went quietly home to live an ordinary life with his parents. Sometimes Joseph did repairs for the fishermen in the towns and villages beside Lake Galilee. Jesus and Mary would go too, because Jesus liked to play with his cousins and the other children who joined in their games.

Sometimes Mary wondered if it had all been a dream; the splendid messenger who told her the news about her child; the excited shepherds who praised God for sending the promised king; the wise men who bowed before her baby; the escape into Egypt. They were such an ordinary family! Yet one day, she knew, Jesus would leave her to do the work God his Father planned: bringing the love of God to everyone.

THE BEGINNING OF JESUS' WORK

So the years passed by until it was time for Jesus to put down the carpenter's hammer and leave his family in quiet Nazareth.

When Jesus was about thirty years old, a man called John came to the River Jordan and began to teach people about God. John had been living in the baking, barren desert.

He was sunburnt and strong. His hair was tangled by the wind and he wore rough clothing made from camel hair. He ate the food of the desert: locusts – creatures like big grass-hoppers – and wild honey. His eyes glowed like the hot sun, and his voice, strong as the wind, brought crowds to the banks of the River Jordan to hear him tell the news of a coming Saviour and king.

'You all do wrong things which make God angry,' John cried. 'Be sorry and start to live new lives and God will forgive you. I shall baptize you here in the river as a sign that you are sorry. There isn't much time. We know God has promised to give us a special king to lead us. He will come

soon and we must be ready for him.'

One day Jesus came to the river and asked to be baptized, too. John knew at once that Jesus was God's promised king. Humbly he baptized Jesus.

As they came up from the water they heard the voice of God himself: 'This is my own dear Son. I am very pleased with him.'

Then Jesus left the crowds on the river bank and went by himself into the desert where nothing grew. There was no tree to shelter him from the scorching sun or the bitter wind that blew at night. Wild animals roamed in the desert. Evil lurked there, and when Jesus had been alone for forty

days, the Devil came to tempt him. The Devil wanted Jesus to use his power to win praise for himself instead of God. He knew Jesus had no food to eat.

First of all he tried to persuade him to turn the desert stones into bread. Jesus refused. 'Men need more than bread to stay alive,' he told the Devil. 'They need to know God's words and obey them, too.'

So the Devil tried again. He took Jesus to the highest tower of the Temple in Jerusalem and said: 'Jump down! Don't be afraid! You won't hurt yourself. The holy writings say that God will send angels to save you from hurting yourself!'

'The holy writings also say that we must not test God,' Jesus replied.

Then the Devil showed Jesus the kingdoms of the world with all their greatness and wealth. 'I will give all this to you if you kneel down and worship me!' the Devil said.

'Go away, Devil!' said Jesus sternly. 'God is the only one to be worshipped.' Defeated, the Devil left Jesus alone, and God sent angels to Jesus to strengthen him after his temptation.

Now Jesus was ready to go back to the people who lived in the towns and villages round about. He made friends with them, helped them and taught them about God.

One day Jesus and some of his friends were invited to a wedding with Mary, Jesus' mother. Everyone enjoyed the party afterwards, but after a while Mary's friend came over to her. 'What shall we do?' she asked. 'We've run out of wine!'

It was a disgrace not to be able to offer wine to the guests all through the wedding. Mary told Jesus what had happened. Then she spoke to the servants. 'My son Jesus will help. Just do whatever he tells you.'

Jesus told the servants to fill six huge jars with water. 'Now take some out and give it to the best man,' he said.

A servant filled a jug and waited anxiously while the best man drank. Would he be angry at being offered water? But the best man smiled. 'This is the best wine I have ever tasted; fancy saving it till last!' he exclaimed. Jesus had turned all the water into wine! Now everyone could enjoy the wedding party.

Then Jesus visited another small town beside Lake Galilee. Two fishermen called Simon and Andrew were on the lake shore mending their nets. Some children came by, and stopped to watch. 'Jesus is coming this way!' the children said. 'We saw him back there along the beach.'

Simon and Andrew looked up quickly. They had met Jesus before and they wanted to talk to him again. Suddenly they heard his voice calling them: 'Simon, Andrew! Come with me! Leave your nets. I want you to help me to tell everyone about God.'

At once the fishermen leapt to their feet. They left their nets behind and followed Jesus. The children watched them go.

Nearby, two more fishermen, James and John, were working with their boat, helping their father. 'Come with us,' Jesus called. 'I need your help, too.' So the two fishermen said goodbye to their father and went with Jesus.

Simon invited them all to come home with him. 'My wife and her mother will be so pleased to see you, Jesus!' he said. Simon did not know that his wife's mother was ill in bed.

'Oh, dear Teacher, I wanted to give you a proper welcome!' she said when she saw Jesus. 'Then I felt so hot and weak I had to lie down.'

Jesus touched the old lady's hand to heal her. She felt better immediately. She got up at once and cooked them all a delicious meal.

That evening crowds of sick people gathered outside Simon's house. Mothers brought their babies. Children led their weak, elderly grandparents. People who couldn't walk were carried, or helped along by friends. Blind people were guided. Some people whose worries and problems made them sick, came to Jesus. People who were possessed by evil spirits came. Jesus helped them

all. He touched the sick and made them well. He drove away the evil spirits. Now all the people knew that God cared about them and had sent Jesus to help them, but some of their leaders felt very angry when they saw how many people followed Jesus.

One of the leaders was called Nicodemus. He loved God and wanted to know more about him. Nicodemus saw how Jesus healed people and taught them. 'This man seems to know God in a special way,' he thought. So Nicodemus decided to speak to Jesus, and one night, after dark, when no one would see, the puzzled leader went to find him.

They talked together for a long time. Jesus answered Nicodemus' questions and explained many things to him. At last Nicodemus went home very thoughtfully. For a long time he told nobody, but secretly he had decided to become a follower of Jesus, too.

All kinds of people, rich and poor, well and sick, old and young, women and men came to Jesus and he helped them all.

Once Jesus and his friends went through a part of the country called Samaria. It was hot, and while the others went to buy food, Jesus rested beside a well. A woman came by for some water. She said nothing to Jesus, for her people and his were enemies and never spoke to one another. Nor did a Jewish man usually speak to a woman whom he met outside her home. To the woman's surprise Jesus asked her to give him a drink of water.

'Why are you asking me?' she exclaimed. Soon they were deep in talk. The woman's amazement grew as Jesus told her about the work God had given him to do. He knew all about her, too, and the wrong things she had done. Greatly impressed she went home and came back with all her friends. She wanted them to meet Jesus, as well.

STORIES JESUS TOLD

Soon large crowds followed Jesus wherever he went and he taught them about God. He always spoke simply. He didn't make things difficult as some of their leaders did. Jesus told amusing, interesting stories, explaining to the people that God loved them very much and they should always try to put God first in everything. Here are some of the stories that Jesus told.

There was once a shepherd who loved his sheep. He would come into the fold, call their names, and lead them away to the best pastures. Sometimes thieves would try to steal the sheep and fierce wolves would attack the flock, but the shepherd would protect them, however great the danger.

'I am like that good shepherd,' said Jesus. 'The people who follow me are like those sheep. I know them and they know me. I look after them, and I give my life to keep them safe.'

Often Jesus used his stories to teach people what God is like. Here is a story about a farmer who had two sons. 'I want to see the world,' thought the younger son. 'When my father is dead, I'll get a share of his goods, but I want some money now. I'll go and ask my father for my share of his things. Then I'll leave home and do whatever I want.'

The farmer felt very sad that his son wanted to leave home, but he loved him, and so he gave him sheep and goats which the young man took to market and sold. With his purse full of money, he set off to find fun and excitement in the big city.

At first he found plenty of fun and a great many friends who invited him to their parties, but when his money was spent, his new friends disappeared, too. No one wanted him without any money. He sold his clothes to buy food, but in the end he had nothing left. He was very hungry, so he left the city and found work on a farm. The farmer sent him to look after the pigs.

As he watched the pigs guzzling their food he wished he could have something to eat, too. He was so hungry he could even have eaten the pigs' bean pods. He thought of his home where no one was ever hungry.

'My father is kind and treats everyone, even the servants, well,' he thought. 'How stupid I am, sitting here starving! I'll go back home. I'll tell my father I'm sorry.' The more he thought about it, the better the idea seemed. He planned what he would say: 'Father, I've done wrong. I've treated you badly, and I've done wrong in God's eyes, too. I'm not fit to be your son any more. Please take me back as one of your servants.'

Feeling happier than he had done for a very long time, the young man made his way home to his father.

Some time later when his father was looking out of the window, he spotted a thin figure, limping along. The farmer stared. Then he raced down the dusty road and flung his arms around his son, who started to say how sorry he was, but the farmer hurried into the house with him, overjoyed to have him home again.

'Bring the best robe and put it on my son,' he called to the servants. 'Give him a ring to wear and sandals, too. Kill the young calf. We'll have a splendid feast!'

God is like the kind father in this story. He forgives those who are sorry for the wrong things they have done and come back to him.

Another story Jesus told was about two very different men who went to pray in the Temple. The first man was a Pharisee, who thought he always kept God's laws. He swept proudly in through the Temple doors and stood where everyone could see him. Loudly he told God how good he was: 'Thank you, God, that I'm better than other people. I'm not like that taxman there. I do everything that pleases you.'

The taxman, who had come very quietly into the Temple, bent his head lower and whispered: 'Have pity on me, God. I've done wrong and I'm sorry.'

Both men went home, but God forgave the taxman and not the Pharisee.

Jesus told the story to teach his friends that God is more pleased with those who know they have done wrong and own up, than with those who think they are good but look down on others.

'If you follow my teaching you are like the wise man who built his house on rock,' said Jesus. 'First he dug away the sandy soil. Then when the rain flooded the valley and autumn storms shook the house, it stood firm for it was built solidly right on the rock.

'Another man built a house nearby, but he didn't dig right down to the rock. So when the valley was flooded the sandy soil was washed away. The house came crashing down in the autumn storms.

'Those who don't follow my teaching are like that,' finished Jesus. 'They can never stand firm when troubles come.'

Here is a story which Jesus told about a robbery.

A traveller journeyed along a lonely road which wound through hills where bands of robbers hid. A gang of thieves attacked him, snatched his bags, stripped off his clothes and beat him up.

Then they ran off, leaving the man badly hurt. He would certainly die if no one helped him, but who would stop on such a dangerous road to help an injured man?

It happened that someone did come along, a priest, on his way to pray to God in the Temple. He saw the man, but he was too frightened to stop. Quickly he walked away on the other side of the road.

Later on the wounded man heard footsteps. He was too weak to shout, but whoever came by would be sure to see him. 'Surely this person will help?' he thought as the footsteps came closer.

The passerby was on his way to serve God in the Temple, too. He looked at the man for a moment, but then he crossed the road as well, and went on his way, leaving the hurt man lying by the road in the hot sun.

At last a Samaritan came by. Jews and Samaritans hated one another, but this man felt sorry for the wounded Jew. He got off his donkey, cleaned the man's cuts with oil and bound them with bandages torn from his own clothes. Then he lifted the man onto his donkey and took him to an inn where he looked after him all night.

Next morning he had to go on with his journey. He gave the innkeeper two silver coins. 'I'll pay you more when I return,' he promised, 'so look after him well.'

'Who do you think really cared for the man?' asked Jesus at the end of his story.

'The Samaritan,' came the reply.

'Then you must go and behave in the same way,' said Jesus.

'Don't worry or be anxious,' Jesus told his friends. 'God will give you everything you need. Did you ever see a flower sit down to spin its beautiful dress? Of course not! Yet see how gaily the flowers grow. Look at the purple anemones, the crocuses, the lovely lilies. Even the wealthiest king of all, King Solomon, who wore splendid robes of deep purple, never put on anything as lovely as one wild flower. Look at the grass, starred with flowers one day, and withered the next. God dresses the ground so wonderfully that he will be certain to give you clothes and food, too. So why don't you just believe that? Expect God to look after you and stop worrying all the time!' he finished.

A farmer set out early one morning to sow his seed. He dipped his hand into the bag he carried and scattered the seed over the ground. Some fell on the path. Birds flew down at once and pecked it up before it could grow on the hard, sun-baked earth of the pathway.

Some seed fell into stony earth where there was only a thin layer of soil. Young shoots sprang up very quickly, but they did not take root in the shallow earth, and as soon as the hot sun came up, the tiny plants dried up and died.

Some of the seed fell among thorns which choked the shoots so that they could not grow. Some seed, though, fell into good soil where it grew and ripened, and stood thick and tall. When the harvest came the farmer was happy, for the good ground gave back thirty, sixty, even a hundred times more corn than he had sown. It was a wonderful harvest!

What a good story, and what a wonderful harvest! But there was a secret meaning which Jesus explained to his friends.

'The seed is our message about God. Remember the hard path? That's like the hearts of some people who never understand and accept what we tell them.

'Other people do understand and are thrilled with the message, but they don't want to do anything too hard. They are like the stony soil with only a thin layer of good earth; when trouble comes they give up easily, blaming God. Other people hear our message but all sorts of worries about money and the problems of everyday life grow up in their minds, too, like the thorns in the story. Then the message about God cannot grow in them.

'Yet the good soil gives a splendid harvest, like people who are so glad about God they tell others too, and lead lives that please him.'

Once there was a shepherd who had a hundred sheep. One day one sheep wandered off. When the shepherd counted his flock he found there were only ninety nine left.

'One of my sheep is lost,' he thought sadly, and he left the ninety nine sheep and searched for the missing one until at last he found it. Filled with joy, he picked up the frightened animal, heaved it on to his strong shoulders and carried it safely back to the flock. Then he led all his sheep back to the fold and called his friends: 'Come on, everyone, let's be happy together because my lost sheep is safely back in the fold.'

This story has a secret meaning, too. People who turn their backs on God and forget about him are like the sheep which was lost. God is like the shepherd who searches for his one lost sheep and is glad to find it, even when he has ninety nine others at home.

PEOPLE MEET JESUS

Jesus made the people very happy with his stories, but the priests were angry at his teaching.

They were angry, too, at the things he did. Once Jesus made a lame man well. The man could not walk at all. He had lain on a mat inside his house for twenty years listening to everything going on around him, but unable to join in. But he did have four good friends, and one day they carried him to Jesus.

As usual, such a large crowd had collected that they could not get near the door of the house where Jesus was. Determined that Jesus should help their friend, the four men scraped a hole in the mud roof, and lowered the lame man through it.

Jesus smiled at the man. 'Everything you have done wrong is forgiven,' he said. 'Get up, now, and walk.' At once, the man stood up and walked out. He hurried home, thanking God.

Everyone was overjoyed, but the priests were angry. 'Only God can forgive people,' they said.

Jesus often made friends with people no one else liked. He even chose a tax collector to be one of his closest followers. The tax collectors worked for the Romans. They took money from the people and paid it over to the Roman rulers. That made people dislike them, but, even worse, many of them cheated people and charged them too much, keeping the extra money for themselves.

One day Jesus went straight up to the table where a tax collector called Matthew was working. 'Follow me,'

he said. Matthew got up at once. He left his money bags and rolls of parchment and hurried away with Jesus. That evening he held a party so that other tax collectors could meet Jesus. Some people were shocked to see Jesus mixing with such dishonest men.

'Dishonest people need me, too,' he said. 'In fact they are the very ones I have come to tell about God, who is ready to forgive us when we are sorry about what we have done wrong.'

It was hard for people to understand why Jesus mixed with those who broke all the Jewish Laws, and they began to call Jesus a law-breaker too, especially when it looked as though he disobeyed the strict laws about the holy Sabbath. This was the name given to the seventh day of their week, Saturday. It was a special day, given to God, when no work could be done.

One Saturday Jesus and his friends were walking through the fields. They felt hungry and picked some wheat. They rubbed the ears and ate the nutty kernels.

Some of the leaders were watching and came over to Jesus at once. 'Your friends are breaking the law! No one is allowed to work on a Sabbath. Picking and rubbing wheat is work!'

Jesus was angry. He knew God made the Sabbath to be a time of rest when people could worship him. The leaders had made up so many rules that keeping the Sabbath Day was a burden, not something to be enjoyed.

Jesus explained this to them, but they were angry too, and would not listen. 'Jesus breaks our laws,' they muttered, and they began to watch him carefully, to see if they could find a way to get rid of him.

On another Saturday Jesus went into the synagogue to pray. There he saw a man with a crippled hand. Jesus knew that if he helped the man the watching leaders would accuse him of breaking the Sabbath law, but Jesus said to them: 'If your sheep falls into a hole, you lift it out at once, even on the Sabbath.' Then he turned to the man. 'Stretch out your hand,' he said, and the man obeyed. At once his hand was well and strong again. Then Jesus' enemies were so angry they started to make plans together to have him put to death.

In one of the small towns beside Lake Galilee there was a synagogue which a Roman officer had built for the Jewish people. The officer was a good, just man, who believed in God. He had a servant whom he treated well and liked very much.

One day the servant became ill. How worried his master was! He told the Jewish synagogue leaders about it, and asked them to fetch Jesus.

Jesus came at once to the house where the officer lived, but before he arrived the officer came to meet him.

'Don't bother to come any further, sir,' the soldier said to Jesus. 'I know you are under God's authority, just as I am under my commander. I give orders, too, and the soldiers under me obey at once. Just give the order and my servant will recover.'

Jesus was amazed. 'I have never met any of my people who believes like this!' he said. 'Go home,' he told the officer. 'What you have believed will indeed happen.' At that very moment the servant became well.

Sometimes Jesus and his friends tried to find quiet places away from the crowds so that they could rest and spend time together. One evening they got into a small boat and set off across Lake Galilee. Jesus was tired and he soon fell fast asleep. Suddenly a fierce wind blew up and huge waves crashed over the sides of the boat. Jesus' friends were terrified and hurried to wake him. Jesus sat up at once. He was not afraid when he saw the tremendous waves. 'Be still!' he told the storm.

At once the wind dropped and the waves grew calm. His friends were amazed. 'Who can this man really be?' they asked one another.

Besides Matthew and the fishermen, Jesus chose seven more men to be his close friends. One day he called them all together and gave them their own work to do. He sent them in twos all through the countryside and told them to tell everyone about God, and heal the sick.

They were not to carry anything with them: no money; no food; no extra clothing; no bag; no shoes — not even a stick to lean on. People they helped would give them what they needed because they were doing God's work. So the twelve men set off. They taught the people about God and made the sick well.

Wherever Jesus went a crowd was sure to try to follow him. Often people simply chased after the little fishing boat if they caught sight of Jesus on board. As soon as he landed they gathered about him. Once this happened Jesus felt so sorry for the people he stayed with them all day.

When evening came his friends asked him to send everyone away to find food, but Jesus said, 'Give them food yourselves.'

Andrew, one of his friends, came forward leading a boy. 'This child has five loaves and two fish,' he said, 'but they won't go very far!'

Quietly Jesus took the basket the boy held out to him. 'Make the people sit down,' he said to his friends. Then he thanked God for the food, and his friends shared it out among the people. There was plenty for everyone, although there were more than five thousand people there.

They were all amazed at Jesus' power. Many of them wanted to make him their king, but Jesus slipped away and found a quiet place where he could pray to God.

Jesus knew that people found it hard to understand what he had really come to do. Even his close friends found it hard to understand when he tried to explain to them that he would be put to death but that God would bring him to life again.

One day Jesus took Simon, James and John into the hills. They climbed a high, lonely mountain and Jesus went ahead to pray. As the fishermen watched they saw that his face was shining with light. His clothes dazzled them with a whiteness brighter than snow in sunshine. Jesus had become splendid with light. Two men stood talking to him. They were Moses and Elijah, two long-dead leaders of the Jewish people. Amazed, Simon called out to Jesus. At that moment a shining cloud covered them and from it came the voice of God himself: 'This is my dear Son. Listen to him!'

The fishermen fell on their faces in fear. When they looked up, the cloud, Moses and Elijah had gone. Only Jesus stood beside them. He spoke to them and they felt less afraid. Slowly they went down the mountain. Now they knew that Jesus really was God's Son, but it was only after he had been raised from death that they understood the meaning of what they had seen.

Some people still refused to believe that Jesus was God's Son, but many did. This is the story of a blind beggar called Bartimaeus who believed in him.

Bartimaeus was sitting at the road-side as usual, begging. Suddenly he heard a huge crowd go tramping by. Their feet scuffed the dust and set it swirling around the blind man. 'What's happening?' he called out.

'Jesus is coming,' cried the crowd.

At once blind Bartimaeus began to shout: 'Help me, Jesus! Help me!' Unkind people told him to be quiet but he went on yelling.

Then someone said: 'Get up! Jesus heard you shouting. He wants you to come to him.' Bartimaeus jumped up and tottered forward to Jesus, his knobbly fingers stretched out in front of him to guide him along.

'What do you want me to do for you?' asked Jesus, gently.

'Oh, Teacher, I want to see!' said Bartimaeus breathlessly, and was overjoyed to hear Jesus say, 'Your faith has made you see.'

The blind man blinked. He looked up and saw the face of Jesus. Joyfully he followed him along the road, singing and laughing as he thanked God.

Blind Bartimaeus was glad that he had met Jesus, but there was a rich man who ran eagerly to see Jesus and

then went away feeling very sad. The rich man was young, well fed and well dressed. His beard was carefully cut and combed. He used perfumes, unlike the poor, the sick and the beggars who crowded around Jesus. Yet there was something the rich man needed, too. He knelt before Jesus and explained what it was. He wanted to go to heaven when he died. 'What must I do?' he asked Jesus.

'You must keep God's commandments,' answered Jesus.

'I have obeyed them all my life, Teacher!'

Jesus looked very lovingly at the young man. 'There is still one thing. Sell your things. Give the money to the poor and follow me.' Jesus spoke warmly, but the young man shook his head. He couldn't bring himself to give up his money. He walked away slowly. He felt very sad and Jesus was sorry, too.

Once two sisters, Martha and Mary, invited Jesus to their house. Martha got on with the cooking, but Mary sat down beside Jesus and listened to him. Poor Martha felt very upset. 'Make my sister come and help me with the work,' she said to Jesus. But he replied, 'Martha, you can cook dinners every day, but Mary is learning about God, and that is best.'

One day when Jesus and his friends came to a village they saw ten men standing by themselves at a safe distance from everyone else. They were ill, and people were afraid that if they came too close they might catch their illness, too. They begged Jesus to make them well. Jesus told them to go and show a priest that they were better – this was what the law said they had to do. As soon as they started off they became well again.

One man came back to say 'Thank you' to Jesus. He told Jesus how pleased he was to be well again. Now he could go back to his family and no longer needed to hide away from everyone.

'There were ten of you, and you're the only one who has come back to say "Thank you",' said Jesus. 'Go back home,' he told the happy man. 'Your faith has made you completely well again.'

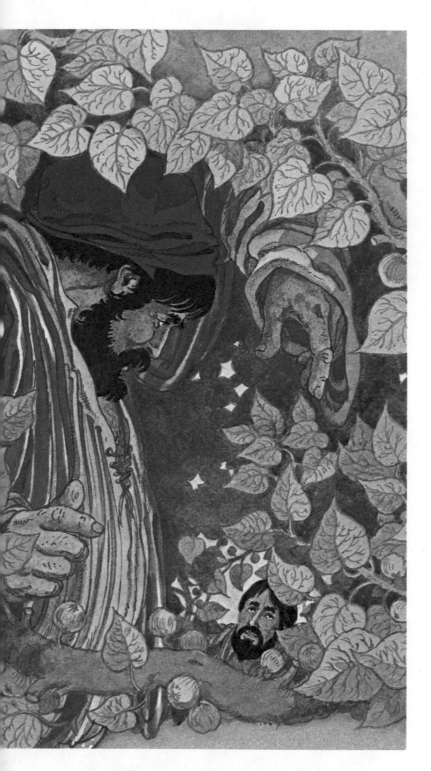

for him. He also knew they all hated him, because he charged everyone too much and kept the money himself. There was no hope of getting through the crowd, and from where he stood he could not see anything at all.

Then he spotted a big tree growing beside the road. Hoping that no one was looking, Zacchaeus clambered up the tree. Now he had a splendid view of Jesus right underneath! Zacchaeus had heard that Jesus made friends with tax collectors and other people who broke the Jewish law, but he couldn't believe it when Jesus called his name: 'Come down, Zacchaeus! I must stay at your house today!'

Joyfully Zacchaeus scrambled down the tree, never minding who saw him. He gave Jesus a splendid welcome, while the crowd waited ouside his house, grumbling. 'What's Jesus doing, mixing with someone like Zacchaeus?'

Then the grumbles changed to loud cheers. Zacchaeus had started giving his things away. 'Come on, everyone!' he shouted. 'Help yourselves. Have I cheated anyone here? Take this, then. Take four times as much!'

When he went back inside, his house seemed bare, but Jesus was there, smiling and pleased. 'Well done,' he said to Zacchaeus, and Zacchaeus felt very happy. He knew that he belonged to God now, and that God had forgiven him all the wrong he had done.

The two sisters, Martha and Mary, had a brother called Lazarus. One day Lazarus became ill and two days later he died. Jesus was far away, but the two sisters sent someone to him with the news. When Jesus arrived at their

Another man felt very glad when he met Jesus. He was a rich man. He lived in a fine, big house and he had plenty of money because he was the chief tax collector. His name was Zacchaeus. As soon as Zacchaeus heard that Jesus was coming to his town, he rushed down the road and joined the crowd already waiting for Jesus. Zacchaeus was a short man. He couldn't see over other people, and he knew that no one would make way

house Martha met him and said, 'If you had been here my brother would not have died. But I know that God will do whatever you ask him.'

'Martha,' said Jesus, 'everyone who believes in me will rise again from death. Do you believe this?' 'Yes,' she answered him firmly. 'Yes, I believe what you say; you are the Son of God.'

Then Mary spoke to Jesus. She, too, was sure that Jesus would have healed her brother. She was crying bitterly, and so were Lazarus' friends. Jesus felt sad and asked them to show him where the body of Lazarus lay.

The body was in a cave which had been closed up with a huge, round stone. Jesus told them to remove the stone. Then he prayed to God and called out loudly, 'Come out, Lazarus!'

Lazarus appeared at the entrance to the cave, alive but still wrapped around with linen cloths.

'Unwind these cloths and let him go,' said Jesus.

Now many more people believed in him, but the priests were furious. They wanted more than ever to arrest Jesus and they watched him carefully, waiting for a chance to seize him.

THE EASTER STORY

Jesus knew very well that his life was in danger, but he knew, too, that it was God's plan for him to die and come to life again. So he went to Jerusalem as usual to celebrate the Passover Festival with his friends.

As they made their way towards the city Jesus had a special surprise for them all: 'You remember our holy writings say that the king whom God is sending will ride into Jerusalem on a donkey? In that village over there you will find a young donkey. Untie him and bring him to me. If anyone complains, say that the Master needs him, and they will let you take him.' Full of excitement two of his friends ran off.

They found the donkey easily, and started to untie him. 'Hey! Stop!' A man poked his head round the doorway. 'What are you doing, taking that donkey?'

'The Master needs it!' said the friends, as Jesus had told them.

'Oh, well, that's different!' said the man. 'Of course you can take the donkey. Treat him carefully, won't you – no one has ever ridden him before.' They untied the donkey and led him to Jesus.

Crowds of people were flocking to Jerusalem for the Passover Festival. Everybody was happy because of the holiday, and when they saw Jesus they cheered with excitement. 'Here comes God's King!' they shouted. People waved green palm branches to greet Jesus. They spread their cloaks over the road for the donkey to walk over as he carried Jesus slowly into the city. On through the streets they went to the beautiful Temple where Jews from all over the world gathered to praise God.

At once Jesus saw something that made him very angry. One of the Temple courts was just like a huge, noisy market place where people could buy birds and animals to offer to God. Lambs bleated loudly, while white doves cooed in cages.

Special coins had to be used inside the Temple, so everyone had to change their money just as though they were going to a foreign country. The money-changers were cheats and kept some of the change.

'God wants the Temple to be a quiet place where people can pray to him!' Jesus said. 'You dealers are wrong. You have made God's Temple like a robber's den! Get out!' He toppled over their tables. Coins rolled in all directions. Then the Temple was in an uproar! Doves flew free from their cages with a flapping of wings. The dealers yelled and raged as Jesus drove them out. Sheep butted one another; calves mooed. The priests and leaders were furious, but every day that week Jesus kept going back to the Temple to teach the people.

His enemies tried to trap him with trick questions. 'Teacher,' they said, politely, 'should we pay taxes to the Romans or not?'

Jesus saw through the trick at once. 'Let me see a coin. Whose name and head are stamped on it?' he asked them.

'The Roman Emperor's,' they replied.

'Then pay the Roman Emperor what is his and pay God what belongs to him,' answered Jesus. Silenced, they slunk away, but Jesus knew that they still watched him closely. As they walked about the Temple, Jesus and his friends watched rich people dropping silver coins into the collecting boxes. They noticed a very poor woman. She was a widow with no husband to help her, and it was plain that she never had enough to eat. She dropped two small copper coins into the box.

'Look, friends,' said Jesus, 'this poor woman has put in far more than all the rich people we have seen.'

'Has she?' his friends asked, amazed.

'Yes,' Jesus answered. 'You see, they gave God only what they thought they could spare. They have plenty of money left, but she is so poor she had only those two coins. She has given God all the money she had.'

Jesus and his friends left the Temple each evening and went out of the city to stay in a little village close by.

There, one evening, a woman called Mary brought expensive perfume and poured it over Jesus' head and feet. As she did so, a wonderful scent filled the room. Mary's tears fell on Jesus' feet as she kissed them and wiped them with her hair.

'What a waste!' came Judas' voice. 'Mary could have sold this perfume and given the money to the poor.'

'No,' said Jesus, 'Mary has done a beautiful thing for me before I die.' Mary was glad, but Judas scowled angrily at Jesus' words. Judas looked after the money for Jesus and the others, and he used to help himself from what was there. If Mary had sold her perfume there would have been more for him to steal. Now every day he grew greedier for money, and he began to be angry with Jesus because he cared for different things.

At last he went to the priests. 'What will you give me if I help you to capture Jesus?' he asked. They counted thirty silver coins into his hand. Judas slipped away, but he was watchful now, waiting for a time when Jesus was alone and his enemies could capture him without any trouble.

Towards the end of the week the time came when Jesus and his friends ate the Passover meal together. They found a secret room in Jerusalem where they could eat together in safety. Their supper was a special kind of bread, and lamb with sauce and herbs. Jesus spoke to them about the love of God.

Then he left the table and took off his long tunic. He tied a towel round his waist, poured water into a bowl, and, just like a servant, went to his friends in turn and washed the dust of the city streets from their feet.

Simon Peter said, 'Lord, you mustn't wash my feet like a servant!'

'I'm washing your feet because I love you, Simon,' said Jesus. 'My friends, I am happy to work for you like a servant. You must be ready, too, to serve one another in humble ways.' Jesus sat down again. 'One of

you is going to hand me over to my enemies,' he said sadly.

'Who could it be?' they wondered anxiously, but Judas knew.

Then Jesus took some bread, broke it and shared it with his friends. 'This is my body, which is given for you,' he said. 'When you break and eat bread together like this you must remember me.' Sad and puzzled, they shared the bread.

Then Jesus passed the cup of wine round among them. 'Drink this, all of you,' he said. 'This is my blood, which will be poured out so that men's sins can be forgiven by God.'

They did not understand. Why did he keep talking about dying when every day crowds followed him and praised him? Sadly they followed him out to a quiet garden, but Judas slipped away.

On the way Jesus warned them

again of all that was to happen. 'I'll stick by you,' declared Simon Peter. 'Even if all the others run away and leave you.'

'Before you hear the cock crow tomorrow morning you will say three times that you do not know me,' said Jesus. 'Pray for me,' he added. Then he went on and prayed alone: 'Father, if it is possible, don't let me go through this terrible death!' His hair stuck to his forehead, wet with sweat. With a great effort he cried out, 'Father, don't do what I want. Do what you know is best.'

He returned to his friends and found them asleep. 'Could you not stay awake?' asked Jesus. 'Get up now. Here come my enemies.' Into the quiet garden came Judas, followed by soldiers and a rough crowd armed with sticks and spears. The chief priests had sent them all to capture Jesus.

'The man I kiss is the one you want,' muttered Judas. He went straight to Jesus. 'Peace, Teacher,' Judas said, and kissed Jesus.

Jesus looked steadily at Judas. 'Why are you here, friend?' he asked gently. 'Have you come to give me away with your kiss?' Then the soldiers grabbed hold of Jesus and held him securely. 'Don't hurt my friends,' Jesus warned them.

Simon Peter, who carried a sword, struck at a slave and cut off his ear.

'Put your sword away, Simon,' said Jesus. 'I shall go with them willingly, for this is the way my Father has chosen for me.' The crowd fell silent. 'Did you have to come with sticks and spears to capture me?' Jesus asked them. 'Day after day I went to the Temple. You all saw me there, but none of you arrested me then.'

He touched the wounded man and healed his ear.

'Now is the time for the powers of darkness to have their way,' Jesus said. The soldiers hurried him roughly

out of the garden. His terrified friends scattered among the trees, leaving Jesus alone in the power of the men who hated him and wanted to kill him.

Now that they had managed to capture Jesus at last, his enemies had to find a reason to have him killed. They asked him questions the whole night long.

They brought in people who told lies about Jesus, but none of their stories agreed. Finally, at dawn, the High Priest asked, 'Are you the Son of God?'

'Yes, I am,' Jesus replied.

'He claims to be God! That's against our holy law!' cried the High Priest.

'He's guilty!' the others agreed. 'He must die.'

Outside in the courtyard Simon Peter, Jesus' friend, stood by the fire. The High Priest's servants noticed him.

'You're one of Jesus' friends,' a servant challenged him.

'Nonsense, I don't even know him,' declared Simon Peter uneasily, but a little later another servant spotted the strong fisherman.

'Hey, this fellow's one of them, too!' he said.

'Me? Certainly not!' lied Simon Peter.

'Come on, you can't fool us! You're from Galilee, too. Your accent gives you away. Of course you were with Jesus.'

'No, I don't know him!' Simon Peter shouted. Beyond the courtyard the first pale streaks of daylight showed in the sky. A cock close by crowed loudly.

Then Simon Peter remembered how Jesus had warned him that before the cock crowed that morning, he would say three times that he did not know Jesus. He rushed outside and cried bitterly.

The Jewish rulers took Jesus to the Roman Governor, a man called Pontius Pilate.

'We've brought you a real trouble-maker,' they warned Pilate. 'He stirs up our people against the Romans. He even calls himself a king!'

Pilate looked at Jesus curiously. 'Are you a king?' he asked.

'So you say,' answered Jesus, and he would not reply to any more of Pilate's questions.

Pilate looked helplessly at his prisoner. He knew Jesus was innocent, but the priests wanted him killed, and the Roman Governor did not dare annoy them, so he led Jesus outside and showed him to all the people. 'You know I always set free one of your prisoners at Passover Festival time,' Pilate told the crowd. 'Here is Jesus. Shall I let him go?'

'No!' shouted the people. 'Free Barabbas instead.' Barabbas was a bandit. Pilate was afraid of the crowd, so, while Barabbas was set free, he handed Jesus over to the soldiers who beat him cruelly. They made a crown from thorny twigs and forced it onto Jesus' head. Then they wrapped a purple cloak round him and bowed to him, jeering, 'Long live the King!'

At last Pilate took Jesus out to the crowd.

'What do you want me to do with this man?' he asked. 'He has done nothing wrong to deserve death.'

'The cross!' yelled the people, persuaded by the priests. 'Let him die on the cross!'

Back in his own stained clothes, Jesus was led away to die. He had to carry his own cross. It was heavy, and his shoulders were torn and bleeding from the soldiers' whips. On the road he stumbled and fell under the weight. Then the soldiers seized a man called Simon, who had come from North Africa to keep the festival in Jerusalem. They forced him to carry Jesus' heavy load. Simon remembered that cross for the rest of his life.

Beyond the city walls was a place called 'Skull Hill'. There they laid Jesus down on the cross and hammered nails through his hands and feet.

Jesus said, 'Father, forgive them. They don't understand what they are doing.'

Two robbers were nailed to crosses on either side of him. The soldiers, to pass the time, threw dice to see who would win the clothes which Jesus wore. A large crowd watched, while their leaders jeered, 'Get yourself off the cross, King!'

One of the robbers joined in and jeered at Jesus, too, but the other said, 'We are both getting what we deserve, but this man hasn't done anything wrong!' Turning his head towards Jesus he said, 'Remember me when you come back as king.'

'Today you shall be in Paradise with me,' Jesus answered, firmly.

It was nine o'clock when they nail-ed Jesus to the cross. At mid-day the sky grew black. Jesus called out into the darkness, 'My God, my God, why have you deserted me?' Some people heard him and wondered if, even now, God would rescue him.

Jesus had little strength left. 'I'm so thirsty!' he gasped. Soldiers soaked a sponge with sour wine and lifted it up to moisten his lips.

'Everything is finished!' Jesus cried. He bowed his head and died.

Two of his secret followers begged Pilate for Jesus' body. They wrapped it in strips of linen cloth and took it to a garden where there was a new grave cut into the rock. Women who had helped Jesus went to the garden, too. They watched the men roll a heavy stone in front of the entrance to the grave, and went home very sadly. The holy Sabbath was just beginning, but on Saturday evening the women got to work preparing perfumes and spices to lay in the linen grave cloths. It was the only way they could show how much they cared for Jesus.

Early on Sunday morning they made their way to the garden where the grave was. To their surprise they saw that the grave stood wide open. They ran to fetch Simon Peter and another friend, John. The two men raced to the grave. It was quite empty. There was no body at all. Only the linen cloths lay on the ground. Puzzled, the men went away, but one of the women, Mary, stayed crying.

'What is the matter? Why are you crying?' a man spoke to her. She thought he must be the gardener.

'Sir,' she said, 'do you know where his body is now?'

'Mary!' said the man, and then she knew. It was Jesus!

'Master!' she exclaimed happily, as her tears melted away.

'Go and tell my friends I am alive,' said Jesus joyfully.

Mary ran back at once to Jesus' friends, but they wouldn't believe her. 'Alive? It can't be true!' they muttered.

That afternoon two of the men left Jerusalem for nearby Emmaeus, talking as they went. A stranger caught up with them. 'What are you discussing?' he asked.

'Haven't you heard about Jesus of Nazareth?' they said. 'We thought he was the one sent by God to help us, but he has been put to death. Now some women are saying he is alive again. Certainly his body has disappeared. It's very puzzling.'

'But don't our holy writings say that God's promised king must die and rise again?' asked the stranger, and he explained many things to them.

They were so interested that they asked him to stay with them. So he went to their house and shared their supper. He took the bread, thanked God and broke it, just as Jesus used to do. Then they saw it *was* Jesus. They were overjoyed, but he disappeared immediately.

The two men rushed straight back

to Jerusalem. They wanted to tell the others, but their friends had their own exciting news to tell – 'Jesus is alive! Simon Peter saw him, too.'

'We know he is alive. He met us on the road and talked to us!' the two men answered.

Suddenly Jesus was in the room with them. They were terrified, but Jesus quickly spoke to them: 'I'm not a ghost. Touch me. You can't touch a ghost!'

Still they could hardly believe it. Yet there he was, smiling, showing the marks in his hands and feet where he had been nailed to the cross.

'Have you any food, friends?' he asked. They gave him some cooked fish, and watched, amazed, as he ate. 'Soon you must go and tell everyone that I died and came alive again so that their sins could be forgiven,' said Jesus. 'But first you must wait until God sends the Holy Spirit to be with you in my place. He will give you the help you need.'

One of Jesus' friends, Thomas, was out when Jesus met the others. He didn't believe their news. 'Unless I actually touch the scars in his hands, I won't believe Jesus is alive!' Thomas said.

Eight days later Thomas was with the others and Jesus came again. 'Look, Thomas,' he said, 'here are the marks of the nails. Touch these scars and believe.'

Thomas fell to his knees. 'You are my Lord and my God!' he declared.

'Thomas, you believe because you can see me,' said Jesus, 'but how happy people will be who believe in me even without seeing me!'

Later, some of Jesus' friends went home to Galilee. One night they went fishing but caught nothing. At day-break someone on the shore called, 'Throw out your net to the right!' They did so, and at once their net was weighed down with fish.

'That's Jesus!' John said to Simon Peter. Simon leapt into the sea to go to him. On the beach Jesus had a fire blazing and some fish ready cooked.

'Bring some more fish,' he said. Simon Peter went back and hauled the heavy net ashore.

'Breakfast's ready!' Jesus called. After breakfast Jesus asked Simon Peter quietly, three times, 'Simon, do you love me?'

'Yes, Lord,' answered Simon Peter each time, remembering sadly how he had lied three times about Jesus.

'Then look after my followers,' said Jesus. Now Simon Peter knew that Jesus still trusted him.

Soon the time came for Jesus to leave his friends and go back to heaven to be with God. One day he and his close friends went out of the city. They climbed a hill. Jesus prayed that his friends would always know God's love and peace.

'You must tell everyone the good news,' Jesus said. 'I am alive for ever and I shall be with you always right to the end of time, just as I told you.' Then Jesus disappeared from their sight.

They would not see him again on Earth, but they knew the Holy Spirit would come and help them.

Returning to Jerusalem they went to the Temple every day to thank God for Jesus. They knew God had sent him to die and come to life again so that everyone who believed in him could be freed from the power of wrong-doing, death and evil.

'Jesus is alive!' they sang, knowing that from then on the whole world would be different.